AF575845

FRANCE

Tracy Vonder Brink

TABLE OF CONTENTS

A Crabtree Seedlings Book

School-to-Home Support for Caregivers and Teachers

This book helps children grow by letting them practice reading. Here are a few guiding questions to help the reader with building his or her comprehension skills. Possible answers appear here in red.

Before Reading:

- What do I think this book is about?
    - *I think this book is about France.*
    - *I think this book is about places to visit in France.*

- What do I want to learn about this topic?
    - *I want to learn about the Eiffel Tower.*
    - *I want to learn what language is spoken in France.*

During Reading:

- I wonder why...
    - *I wonder why there are so many museums in Paris.*
    - *I wonder why the Loire Valley in France has more than 300 castles.*

- What have I learned so far?
    - *I have learned that Paris is the capital of France.*
    - *I have learned that Notre-Dame de Paris is a famous church in Paris that is more than 800 years old.*

After Reading:

- What details did I learn about this topic?
    - *I have learned that the Eiffel Tower has more than 1,000 steps that go from the bottom to the top.*
    - *I have learned that the Arc de Triomphe is a monument that honors French soldiers.*

- Read the book again and look for the vocabulary words.
    - *I see the word* ***monuments*** *on page 6, and the word* ***lavender*** *on page 18. The other glossary words are found on pages 22 and 23.*

France is a country.

It is in **Europe**.

Paris is the **capital** of France.
A river flows through Paris.
It is called the Seine.

Most people who live in France speak French.

Paris has many **monuments**.

The Arc de Triomphe honors French soldiers.

The Eiffel Tower is tall.

More than 1000 steps go from the bottom to the top.

It also has seven elevators.

Gustave Eiffel created the tower for the 1889 World's Fair.

Notre-Dame de Paris is a famous church in Paris.

It is more than 800 years old.

Paris has many museums.

The Louvre is the largest art museum in the world.

It holds paintings, **statues**, and more.

Mont-Saint-Michel is an island in northern France.

A famous church sits on its top.

The Loire Valley is in **central** France.

It has more than 300 castles.

Chambord is the largest castle there.

Provence is an area in southern France.

It has mountains and beaches.

Provence also has fields of **lavender**.

Lavender smells light and fresh. It is used in some soaps, lotions, and candles.

Markets in Provence are full of good food.

Visiting France is fun!

RPH-onions

Glossary

capital (KAP-i-tl): The city where the government of a country or a state is located

central (SEN-truhl): Near, in, or at the center

Europe (YOOR-up): The continent between the Atlantic Ocean and Asia

lavender: (LA-vuhn-dr): A sweet-smelling plant with light purple flowers

monument (MAHN-yoo-muhnt): Something that is put up to remember a person or an event

statue: (STA-choo): A figure of a person or an animal made by an artist from a hard material such as metal or stone

Index

About the Author

Tracy Vonder Brink

Tracy Vonder Brink loves to visit new places. She once spent a summer in France and enjoyed a weekend in Paris. She lives in Cincinnati with her husband, two daughters, and two rescue dogs.

Written by: Tracy Vonder Brink
Designed by: Under the Oaks Media
Proofreader: Janine Deschenes
Production coordinator and Prepress technician: Tammy McGarr
Print coordinator: Katherine Berti

Photographs:
Shutterstock: Catarina Belova: cover, p. 7; V_E: p. 3; MarinaD_37: p. 5, 21; Ron Martinez: p. 9; Gurgen Bakhshetyan: p. 11; photosmatic: p. 12-13; milosko50: p. 15; Captblack76: p. 16-17; StevanZL: p. 19

Crabtree Publishing

crabtreebooks.com 800-387-7650

In Canada: We acknowledge the financial support of the Government of Canada through the Canada Book Fund for our publishing activities.

Hardcover 978-1-0396-4458-8
Paperback 978-1-0396-4649-0

Printed in the U.S.A./112023/PP20230920

Published in Canada
Crabtree Publishing
616 Welland Avenue
St. Catharines, Ontario
L2M 5V6

Published in the United States
Crabtree Publishing
347 Fifth Avenue
Suite 1402-145
New York, NY 10016

Written by: Tracy Vonder Brink
Photo Credits: Shutterstock: Catarina Belova: cover, p. 7; V_E: p. 3; MarinaD_37: p. 5, 21; Ron Martinez: p. 9; Gurgen Bakhshetyan: p. 11; photosmatic: p. 12-13; milosko50: p. 15; Captblack76: p. 16-17; StevanZL: p. 19

Library and Archives Canada Cataloguing in Publication
Available at the Library and Archives Canada

Library of Congress Cataloging-in-Publication Data
Available at the Library of Congress